Made in United States
North Haven, CT
10 June 2023

37589595R00057